Terrence Malick

An Annotated Bibliography of

Dissertations and Theses

Elizabeth J. Hester

_____

Hester, Elizabeth J.

Terrence Malick: An annotated bibliography of dissertations and theses/Elizabeth J. Hester

p. cm.

1. Malick, Terrence, 1945 -- Criticism and Interpretation. 2. Film. I. Title.

PN 1998.3 M3388 H713

791.43023

ISBN 978-1-935779-04-9

Table of Contents

Asenas, Jennifer.

Redressing the Vietnam Syndrome: Variations on a Just War Theme in Three Post-Vietnam World War II Films. M.A. thesis, California State University, Long Beach, 2002.

War films both reflect and sculpt a community's view on war. Films about the Vietnam War shattered American's trust in their warriors because they were unable to overcome war's scene or control the weapons of war, but more importantly, American's questioned the purpose of war. Popular culture has seemingly rehabilitated the image of the warrior, but has yet to remedy our culture's belief in the efficacy of war. This thesis argues that the reemergence of World War II films, specifically *Saving Private Ryan*, *The Thin Red Line*, and *Pearl Harbor,* remedy the Vietnam Syndrome by reaffirming the possibility of a just war.   (Author abstract – Asenas)

Bathori, Jon E.

Warum Krieg? The Stricken Field and Freud's Other Scene in Terrence Malick's Film "A Thin Red Line". Psy.D. dissertation, The Wright Institute, 2007.

Albert Einstein's petition to Sigmund Freud regarding the cause and means of deliverance from warfare is used to articulate a response from the perspective of the Freudian Field that includes a savoir. A survey of war demonstrates that beyond privileged ubiquity in all cultures, the primary feature of battle is violent excess: an attempt to guarantee the pleasures of death and purposeful cruelty. The ascendancy of atrocity in modernity indicates that the symbolic limits to the toxic effects of jouissance and the drive have degraded. The suspension and subsequent transgression of the taboo against murder creates the conditions for violence without limit that challenge the basic pact of coexistence. War is identical to the experience of the psychoanalytic clinic, in as much as their shared elements--the registers of experience, the passions of the drive and the work of death brought by jouissance -- are at play. The dysregulation of the human organism occasioned by compulsive quest for das Ding (the object of the drive) and jouissance, breaches the limits of the pleasure principle, corroding the social link. Psychoanalysis demonstrates that beyond transgression, morality and the defiles of the Other, an ethical position must be taken for jouissance given the tension created between the vital needs of satisfaction and the exigencies of coexistence. The specificity of the masculine position presents as an obligation to represent the phallus beyond narcissism, and in the face of the failure of the symbolic. War further challenges to the symbolic means to drain off the excess of jouissance and fully face the arbitrary, death, the Real and the void at the center of human existence. Terrence Malick's film, *A Thin Red Line*, is examined as an example of an aesthetic experience which successfully presents all of the elements above and the links the stakes of masculinity with the experience of war as the subject of the unconscious struggling to cope not only with the exigencies of battle field but as the stricken field beyond the pleasure principle. Implications for clinicians are discussed in light of the work of the drive and ethics. (Author abstract – Bathori)

Brickman, Barbara Jane.

Looking for My Heart's Desire: Popular Cinema and the Post-War Adolescent Imaginary. Ph.D. dissertation, University of Rochester, 2005.

Looking for My Heart's Desire: Popular Cinema and the Post-war Adolescent Imaginary examines representations of adolescent spectatorship and fantasy in post-World War II literature and "teen films." While most critics of the teen film genre find that the films, overall, work to reinforce the bond between father and son and through that bond to reassert patriarchal order, I would argue that there are several elements working within the films and within spectatorship that offer serious challenges to such claims. This investigation of adolescent spectatorship and fandom offers a new view of the teen audience, which is often regarded with suspicion and anxiety or dismissed as passive captives to mass media's consumer messages. I propose not only that these young spectators might be more critical readers and fans of films than previous work has claimed, but also that the narratives themselves contain refusals and rewritings of the conservative resolutions of traditional Hollywood films. Fantasy provides for these viewers a means for re-vision and play not foreclosed by traditional plots or constrained by gender or sexual norms. Instead, these young spectators transform their obsessive film viewing into a creative act of their own outside of the theater. That these fantasies play out violent refusals of authority and the law marks them as both typically adolescent and darkly radical. In Chapter One, I examine one particular male adolescent spectator, Holden Caulfield, to suggest a potential instability in that spectator, his turn to male masochism, and the refusal of paternal legacy which results from the process. Chapter Two turns to Holly in Terrence Malick's *Badlands*, a female adolescent spectator and fan whose omniscient voiceover and controlling vision not only show that female authorship is possible but also expose a female mind at play, sometimes cruelly, with popular culture, Hollywood stars, and patriarchal order. With Pauline Parker and Juliet Hulme, as depicted in *Heavenly Creatures*, Chapter Three imagines the resistant viewer and fan through a couple, who together rewrite popular culture through shared fantasy and creative production. Finally, Chapter Four considers the possibility of these revisions being transferred to the screen by young filmmakers. (Author abstract – Brickman)

Feldman Nebenzahl, Bernardo.

The Narrative Power of Sound: Symbolism, Emotion and Meaning Conveyed through the Interplay of Sight and Sound in Terrence Malick's "Days of Heaven." Ph.D. dissertation, University of California, Los Angeles, 2000.

Days of Heaven, written and directed by Terrence Malick, is a movie which utilizes images and sounds as substantial narrative tools. This thesis examines some of the particular ways in which image and sound combine to convey symbolism, emotion, and meaning. It makes reference to several biblical and literary examples that serve as archetypal models for Malick's film. It focuses on the means by which Mr. Malick shapes these archetypal concepts into a complex cinematic experience. The author's main objective is to interpret the complex manners in which sound interacts with all other dramatic devices that make up a film. Therefore, a strong emphasis has been placed on the role of speech, music, and sound effects as devices to convey intellectual significance and artistic expression.The paper concludes with a brief retrospective and reevaluation of various artistic developments from the early twentieth century which utilize image and sound in innovative ways. At one time were considered esoteric, abstract imagery and non-musical sounds are gaining broad acceptance amonst mainstream audiences through their frequent use on film, television, and other media. It is the author's aim to encourage the analysis of dynamic interactions between image and sound with an emphasis on their psychological connotations in order to refine their effective use within the performing and visual arts. (Author abstract – Feldman Nebenzahl)

Harris, Adam.

Identity and Asphalt: The Search for Celebrity in "Bonnie and Clyde" and "Badlands." M.A. thesis, University of Wyoming, 1995.

This thesis develops a model which can be used to analyze films of the outlaw-couple-on-the-road genre. I look at two early films of the genre, *Bonnie and Clyde* and *Badlands*, in this work. Other, later films of the genre owe much to these primary outlaw couple films. My model proposes four basic areas of investigation for examination of this genre: the nature of the outlaw couple story; where the desire for celebrity comes from and how it show up in films; the character traits and skills necessary to become an outlaw; and, the largest section, the celebrity image creation system that operates throughout the films. (Author abstract – Harris).

Jordan, Tibe Patrick.

A War on Two Fronts: Steven Spielberg's "Saving Private Ryan" and Terrence Malick's "The Thin Red Line". M.A. thesis, Florida Atlantic University, 2001.

In 1998 *Saving Private Ryan* and *The Thin Red Line* debuted in theatres and critics in the popular press were quick to discuss the revival of the World War Two film and to classify both films within this genre. Through an examination of genre, art cinema, the styles of the Steven Spielberg and Terrence Malick, and a close textual analysis of both films, this thesis argues that *Saving Private Ryan*, although updating generic conventions of violence through its opening segment, quickly turns traditional in its depiction of plot, character, masculinity, and nation. *The Thin Red Line*, however, combines conventions of the war film with elements of art cinema, producing a film that popular critics often labeled in an inadequate or incomplete manner, creating inappropriate generic expectations among viewers. (Author abstract – Jordan)

Rosadiuk, Adam.

Film and Philosophic Experience: Terrence Malick's "The Thin Red Line". M.A. thesis, Concordia University, Canada, 2006.

Central to Terrence Malick's 1998 film *The Thin Red Line* is the lightning strike of insight. Insight: a potentially life-altering phenomenon, a rare melding of language, image, and feeling. Insight: a temporality joining the seductiveness of memory, the perceived purity of the moment, and the threat of insight's decay. This thesis is about the problem of insight, and explores cinema's intervention into the motivation, structure, and representation of this phenomenon as philosophy. Malick's drama of American soldiers struggling to survive the Battle of Guadalcanal depicts a crucible of private insight and compulsive public philosophy through a unique cinematic aesthetic pitched between the sublime and the banal. My discussion centers on Malick's use of 'linguistic' figurative tropes and their interaction with Malick's 'visual' cinematic events: a meeting of two forms of expression which reinvigorates the longstanding 'quarrel' between philosophy and poetry, tests the tension between visual and verbal discourses, and gives expression to the wonder, desire, inequality, and disappointment at the center of the experience of insight. By looking at some of the strategies of philosophic communication experimented with by Plato, Thomas Hobbes, Jean-Jacques Rousseau, Friedrich Nietzsche, Martin Heidegger, and Walter Benjamin this thesis understands Malick's work as one that renews fundamental questions about the nature of both private philosophic experience and the public mediums through which it is communicated. *The Thin Red Line* is a unique expression of what is at stake in the meeting of film and philosophy---as well as a stunning artistic achievement---and deserves a thorough analysis. (Author abstract – Rosadiuk).

Ross, Angela M.

The Princess Production: Locating Pocahontas in Time and Place. Ph.D. dissertation, University of Arizona, 2008.

My dissertation, *The Princess Production: Locating Pocahontas in Time and Place*, critically evaluates the succession of representations of Pocahontas since her death in 1617. Pocahontas has become the prototypical "Indian Princess," through which the indigenous "other" is mapped onto Eurocentric constructions of gender and race, and subsequently transformed into the object of desire to be colonized. Chapter One begins with an introduction to the Pocahontas myth, and continues with an overview of the representation of Native Americans in cinema. Given that Native Americans have been the subject of the romanticization of the passing frontier, then the image of Pocahontas, standing in for the gendered "virgin" frontier, has been problematically used to represent American nationhood. In the second chapter, I investigate the commodification of the image of Pocahontas, by way of a critical assessment of Disney's *Pocahontas* (1995). Due to its extreme popularity and plethora of commercial tie-ins, this animated film was able to cement mainstream attitudes of Native Americans and especially of indigenous women. Critical discussion, however, was ameliorated through "politically correct" associations of Indians with ecological balance and moral purity versus European decadence. I analyze the symbolic association of Pocahontas with nature in Chapter Three, particularly in Terence Malick's recent film *The New World* (2005), where this association is most blatant. Malick has been heavily influenced by such philosophers as Martin Heidegger, and his resulting romantic and pantheistic vision clouds gender difference and racial antagonism. The image of Pocahontas in The New World, therefore, simply becomes a signifier for the grand impersonal workings of Nature. Finally, in Chapter Four, I discuss attempts by indigenous writers and groups to reappropriate Pocahontas for Native Americans, and I conclude that this is of strategic importance for transforming Indian identity. Since the image of Pocahontas has played such a large role in the shaping of mainstream attitudes and government policy toward Native Americans, then retrieving it from its colonial legacy will go a long way toward preserving Indian culture and identity in the future. (Author abstract – Ross)

Rybin, Steven M.

The Historical Thought of Film: Terrence Malick and Philosophical Cinema. Ph.D. dissertation, Ohio University, 2009.

Previous scholarly work on the director Terrence Malick has argued that his films - *Badlands* (1973), *Days of Heaven* (1978), *The Thin Red Line* (1998) and *The New World* (2005) - are, in varying ways, philosophical. This assessment is usually made via an analysis of the films in relation to a single philosophical metatext (frequently the work of Martin Heidegger) that transcends the concrete historical situation of both the given film and the historically existing viewer. This study seeks to intervene in this critical literature by theorizing an approach for understanding Malick's films as works that do not merely illustrate already articulated philosophical themes but that rather function, in dialogue with the spectator, as an invitation to generate creative and historically situated meaning. The film medium, this study argues, is uniquely philosophical in that it exists in time (via the gradual entropy of the celluloid film print) as does the finite, historically embodied spectator. Malick's cinema, I argue, reflects poetically upon the finite nature of both the film medium and the viewing subject through films that depict subjective experience in the historical past. Rather than construct a theoretical methodology that will then be "applied" to the films, the study uses its first three chapters to construct a propadeutic (in philosophy, a preparatory framework) that in the remaining chapters inform an exploration of the philosophical thought that Malick's four films encourage. The first chapter of this study places the dissertation's framework in critical debates about the use and function of philosophy in relation to film. The second and third chapters then illustrate in greater detail the project's own approach. The second chapter uses the work of D.N. Rodowick, Gilles Deleuze, Stanley Cavell and others to suggest that in watching films we are led to reflect upon what we value as existential, becoming spectators. The third chapter builds upon the phenomenology of Vivian Sobchack in order to suggest how the temporality of film experience emerges through film space. In the final four chapters, I use the insights of the propadeutic to craft a philosophically informed critical analysis of Malick's four films. This analysis demonstrates not only the philosophical value of the director's oeuvre, but also functions as a case study demonstrating the larger value of philosophy and existential phenomenology to the critical

study of Malick and film in general. (Author
abstract – Rybin)

Smihula, John Henry.

"Where a Thousand Corpses Lie": Critical Realism and the Representation of War in American Film and Literature since 1960. Ph.D. dissertation, University of Nevada, Reno, 2008.

This dissertation examines the anti-war, anti-militarist tradition of American literature and film from Joseph Heller's *Catch-22* (1961) to the most recent documentaries about the ongoing Iraq War. This dissident, deeply humanist tradition has been, in Western art, a central feature of critical realism since Stendhal and Tolstoy, and it continues in such works as Oliver Stone's film *Salvador* (1986) and Anthony Swofford's memoir *Jarhead* (2003). Studies of realism have typically emphasized epistemology and methodology, the revaluation or devaluation of canonical authors, and either realism's obsolescence or continuance in contemporary authors; few studies of realism, however, have argued explicitly and cogently for realism, and none have, to my knowledge, argued for the significance of the realist representation and deromanticization of war. But this is an argument I make. In our time of war, and of the derealization of war--when war is rendered all but invisible and bloodless--I believe it is crucial to revalue and revalorize critical realism. Since realism was historically a reaction to romanticism, I begin my project by comparing two films that portray World War II, our most romanticized and mythologized war: Steven Spielberg's romantic and nationalist *Saving Private Ryan* (1998) and Terrence Malick's realist riposte *The Thin Red Line* (1998). By explicating Malick's critical realization of war--its horror, its senselessness, its insidious propagation--I demonstrate that realism's anti-romanticism and resolute fidelity to empirical fact make it particularly effective in revealing the reality of war. This imperative of realism is even bolder in Heller's satiric and subversive novel *Catch-22,* which is the subject of my next chapter. I then proceed to the Vietnam War and two radical and obscure returned veteran films, *Twilight's Last Gleaming* (1977) and *Cutter's Way* (1981), both of which are doleful reflections on the undemocratic nature of post-war American society. I continue with the U.S. covert war against El Salvador in the 1980s, a noche obscura that Joan Didion (*Salvador,* 1983), Oliver Stone, Manona Wali and Pamela Cohen (*Maria's Story,* 1990) seek to illumine or realize in their respective works. The final war I address is that in Iraq, and I do so through Swofford's memoir, the short-lived 2005 television series *Over There,* and Sinan Antoon's documentary film *About Baghdad* (2004). Each of these chapters, and texts, manifests a different dimension or additional

distinction of critical realism, so that by the end

of my study the reader should understand, and

appreciate, the special and perduring power of

critical realism to lay bare the terrible

phenomenon of war. I assert that today the

stronghold of critical realism is documentary

film, and I close my dissertation with an analysis

of this genre by focusing specifically on Spike

Lee's *When the Levees Broke* (2006), Peter Davis's

Hearts and Minds (1974), and my own *Hidden in

Plain Sight* (2003). (Author abstract – Smihula)

Soliman, Moheb.

Circumnavigating the Great Lakes by Land and Writing Towards an Aesthetics and Ethics of Nature and Sociality. M.A. thesis, University of Toronto, Canada, 2008.

This thesis explores the extent to which natural geography affectively orients sociality and subjectivity through the site of the Great Lakes region. It delineates this discrete space and potential through initially questioning the fixing of nature in Henri Lefebvre's legacy and geographic and ecological discourses. Based on a another project conducted in summer 2007 circumnavigating the Great Lakes by land and writing - poetry, prose and images of which are presented, this thesis conceives an aesthetics of approaching and living with natural space on its own terms. These are articulated through an inquiry of the sublime and disinterestedness in the films Werner Herzog and Terrence Malick.

These ideas finally challenge a body of Great Lakes literature and theories of representationality and 'the gaze' in tourism studies through an emerging ethics of affect, attentiveness, and difference in nature and its imperatives, which is the central contribution of this thesis. (Author abstract – Soliman)

Whish, Bryan.

Euro-Americentric Rhetoric and the Hollywood Indian : A Cultural Critique of the Missing and the New World. M.A. thesis, Northern Arizona University, 2007.

Native Americans have been depicted on film since the beginning of motion pictures. From the beginning to the present, the images of Native Americans have changed very little. It seems that the same stereotypes and imagery are used time and again. Some of these stereotypes include; savage, noble, warrior and princess. Also present in these films is the inevitable white hero. The plot typically revolves around the white hero, making the Native Americans in the film nothing more than moving set pieces, or at the very least, secondary characters or sidekicks. This study is a cultural critique of two contemporary films about Native Americans. *The Missing* and *The New World* are films by two prominent directors,

Ron Howard and Terrence Malick, respectfully. Both filmmakers claim that their films are "authentic" in terms of the depiction of Native Americans. Though these filmmakers claim to be authentic, they both fall into many of the same stereotypes as earlier films. This thesis is not about what stereotypes of prevalent in these films. Rather, this thesis asks the question, why do filmmakers return to such stereotypical depictions even when they claim to reject such archetypes?The white man's burden appears to answer this question. This study utilizes theories from Stuart Hall's cultural studies and George Gerbner's cultivation theory to critique these two films from a Native American Cultural point of view. (Author abstract – Whish)

Wondra, Janet.

American Medusa, American Sphinx: The Female Gaze and Knowledge in Modern Fiction and Film. Ph.D. dissertation, Louisiana State University, 1998.

Two major arguments define this study, the first being that the gaze, a concept borrowed from film theory, provides a productive approach to many literary texts, whether central to the canon, like *The Sound and the Fury* and *The Great Gatsby*, or relatively new to critical attention, like Nella Larsen's *Passing*. Locating and following the gaze enables literary critics to bring into focus the power relations within narratives and the scopic negotiations by which hierarchies of privilege are established and maintained. Second, the study both argues and demonstrates that feminist film theory has prematurely closed important avenues of investigation by assuming that each text affords only one gaze and that this gaze is male. Through readings of literary texts and films including *Days of Heaven, Rear Window, Mata Hari, Pinky,* and both versions of *Imitation of Life,* I argue that what gives many narratives their distinctive shape is the battle among multiple gazers for dominance in looking relations. Through attention to process--the struggle--rather than end product--the denouement--the gaze is revealed as a site of complex negotiations relating to gender but also to race, sexual orientation, age, and class. In their multiplicity, their struggle to position themselves with respect to others who look, and their disruption or assertion of hierarchy, multiple gazers are important not just in themselves, however, or in the power they lend critics to read narratives anew. Rereading the gaze, especially the female gaze, opens up for spectators and readers a variety of opportunities for identification, including the possibility of identifying with contradiction itself. Integral to this study is an examination of the interaction between looking and knowing, for the gaze is used to gather information but also to police the knowledge of others through surveillance. While the gaze may be both a method for accumulating power and a badge of supremacy, the dominant gazer's position is made precarious by the inductive problem: no matter how much one looks or knows, it can never be enough. Consequently, the battle for a dominant gaze continues, multiplying the possibilities for new narratives, cinematic and literary. (Author abstract – Wondra)

Locating Dissertations and Theses

A. Purchase

Many of the dissertations and theses listed in this bibliography are available for purchase through UMI Dissertation Express:

> http://disexpress.umi.com/dxweb

By Fax:

> 800-864-0019

By Mail:

> 789 E. Eisenhower Parkway, P.O. Box 1346, Ann Arbor, Michigan 48106-1346 800-521-3042

B. Interlibrary Loan

Dissertations and theses may also be requested through Interlibrary Loan via your local public, college or university library.

www.ingramcontent.com/pod-product-compliance
Lightning Source LLC
Chambersburg PA
CBHW060101050426
42448CB00011B/2565